Why the Jewish People?

Understanding Replacement Theology & Antisemitism

Thomas Fretwell

Why the Jewish People?

Understanding Replacement Theology & Antisemitism

First printed: 2021

Cover design and layout by: Sarah Fretwell

Printed by: Bishops Printers Ltd, Portsmouth

ISBN: 9781916876811

Published by: Ezra Foundation Press, UK

Please visit our website for more details

www.ezrafoundation.org

Acknowledgements

There are a number of people who have helped me considerably in the completion of this project to whom I would like to express my thanks. Firstly, my wife Sarah for doing a wonderful job with the design of the book and cover. Jeff Cuozzo, for getting behind the vision of the project and supporting it in multiple ways throughout the process. To Philip Bell who did an amazing job with the initial editing on the first manuscript. To all those who kindly read the draft manuscript, provided thoughtful suggestions, and wrote endorsements: Dr. Mitch Glaser, Dr. Daniel Nessim, and Rev. Alex Jacob. Also, to those who proofread the manuscript in its final stages: Charlotte Beveridge and Andrew Fretwell.

Endorsements

I highly recommend Thomas Fretwell's book, *Why the Jewish People?* This effort is comprehensive and covers the biblical, historical, and contemporary material that pertain to this important topic. The purpose of the book is to present reasonable, winsome, and biblical material to counterbalance the teaching usually entitled replacement theology or more classically, Supersessionism. Thomas does an excellent job in summarizing the various teachings of the church fathers on this topic and his response is clear and reasonable showing how these church fathers are correct in many areas, but their writings are also laden with a host of theological misconceptions regarding the role of the Jewish people and God's plan for Israel. Thomas also engages with what contemporary theologians suggest in their interpretations of some key New Testament passages used to affirm the veracity of replacement theology. This book, though brief, will take some time to read and will require careful thought and an open Bible. The journey is worth it!

Dr Mitch Glaser,

President, Chosen People Ministries (New York)

Why the Jewish People? forensically explores replacement theology and provides clear definitions alongside outlining key historical and theological developments within replacement theology and associated anti-Semitic actions and attitudes.

The concluding segment, in which he engages with nine New Testament texts which sometimes are used in error to provide a degree of support for replacement theology, is in my mind extremely well done, and this will hopefully become a valuable entry point to help equip many Bible teachers and preachers.

Rev Alex Jacob M.A., M.Phil,

CEO The Churches Ministry Among Jewish People (CMJ UK)

Why the Jewish People? Addresses an important question for our time in this post-holocaust world where Israel has become the thriving Jewish State that it is. *Why the Jewish People?* shows how replacement theology has fed antisemitism and is being used purposely to fuel anti-Zionism today and provides helpful and illuminating correctives to oft misunderstood verses mistakenly used to teach it.

Dr Daniel Nessim,
Author of *Torah for Gentiles? What the Jewish Authors of the Didache Had to Say*

There are many in the church today who do not even know what the term replacement theology means and yet they adhere to it. I believe there is so much confusion in the church regarding this topic which is based on the traditions of men. Thomas does an excellent job of bringing clarity and understanding to this challenging issue in a simple and uncomplicated way, that any and all who read it will be enlightened.

Pastor Jeff Cuozzo,
UK & European Coordinator Behold Israel

Contents

May all who hate *Zion*
be put to shame and
turned backward.

Psalm 129:5

1

Understanding Replacement Theology & Antisemitism

The Scroll of Fire

Nestled deep in the hills surrounding Jerusalem lies a silent but living testimony to one of the most tragic events in human history. The Martyrs Forest is the largest memorial to the Holocaust in the world: a forest comprised of over six million trees. There are four and a half million pine trees – representing the adults who perished in the Nazi genocide between 1941 and 1945, and one and a half million cypress trees to account for the precious children that were lost at this time. A stunning yet poignant testimony to hatred and death, but also to new life. Standing as if designed to represent the heart of this living, breathing testimony, are The Scrolls of Fire, planted atop the forest's highest hill. These are two eight-feet-tall bronze sculptures that depict the history of the Jewish people through two events: The Holocaust and the rebirth of Israel. Or to look at it another way, it is a monument to commemorate death and celebrate life. The monument itself takes the form of two rolled-up scrolls, resembling the scrolls (megillah) of the Torah, a gesture to the nation's identity as "the people of the book".

The right-hand scroll is decorated with images of tragic events which occurred during the course of the Holocaust. You can see Jews being marched off to the concentration camps by faceless figures, recognizable as Nazis by their distinctive helmets. The faces have been left off in all likelihood to portray the inhumanity of what transpired. Following the images around the scroll we see the Warsaw ghetto and those who fought in the uprising. There is barbed wire and bodies folded on top of one another. We see survivors leaving

By רכייט ישיבא ר"ד:סוליץ, CC BY 2.5.

the camps with their eyes lifted to the heavens. A ship is carrying survivors back to the Land of Israel. An Olive tree has branches resembling human bodies, the artist intending to convey the theme of renewal and re-birth. Just as a tree grows new branches, the people of Israel will now grow in their homeland once again.

At the base of each scroll is a small memorial space with two scriptures engraved at the base:

Therefore prophesy and say to them, 'Thus says the Lord GOD, Behold, I will open your graves and cause you to come up out of your graves, My people; and I will bring you into the land of Israel.

...

I will put My Spirit within you and you will come to life, and I will place you on your own land. Then you will know that I, the LORD, have spoken and done it, declares the LORD.

Ezekiel 37:12,14

These verses come from a famous prophecy that Ezekiel gives concerning the future restoration of his people. The theme is clearly life from death, in keeping with the motif represented by The Scrolls of Fire. The artist responsible for this monument, Warsaw-born Nathan Rapoport, is himself a Holocaust survivor. He has inscribed his own epithet at the memorial:

> "My words have been made of bronze and stone.
> They are silent, heavy and long-lasting."

In the same way much of what this booklet discusses will consist of heavy words that, I trust, will leave a long-lasting impression upon the soul of the reader. As we chart the relationship between Israel and the Church, we will encounter some stark reminders that the Church has many dark periods in its past. The events of the Holocaust may be a matter of historical record, but for many they remain an abstract peculiarity of history. However, for the Jewish people, those events are seared into the collective consciousness of the nation. Nevertheless, the Holocaust did not appear in a vacuum. There were events that precipitated this vulgar outburst of hatred and antisemitism. A long history of Jew hatred exists throughout the world and had taken root in European culture. Tragically, much of this was conducted under the guise of Christianity.

Yellow star of David, CC BY 2.5.

What is Replacement Theology?

Entire volumes have been written, devoted to explaining the complex relationship between Israel and the Church. This relationship has really alternated between two models: replacement and restoration. The focus of this booklet will primarily be on critiquing the former. It is vital that the Church understands what this view teaches and the consequences that often accompany it. The replacement view, commonly known as 'replacement theology' is sometimes given the more academic title 'supersessionism'. In its broadest sense these terms are given to the view that the Church has replaced (or superseded) Israel in the future plan of God. In this view the covenantal promises regarding Israel's future have now been transferred to the Church, which has become the new 'spiritual Israel'. Theologian Walter Kaiser Jr. puts it this way:

> "Replacement theology declared that the church, Abraham's spiritual seed, had replaced national Israel in that it had transcended and fulfilled the terms of the covenant given to Israel, which covenant Israel has lost because of disobedience."[1]

Premillennial Bible scholar Michael Vlach provides a comprehensive description of classical supersessionism as follows:

"Supersessionism, therefore, appears to be based on two core beliefs: (1) the nation of Israel has somehow completed or forfeited its status as the people of God and will never again possess a unique role or function apart from the church, and (2) the church is now the true Israel that has permanently replaced or superseded national Israel as the people of God. In the context of Israel and the church, supersessionism is the view that the NT church is the new and/or true Israel that has forever superseded the nation Israel as the people of God."[2]

Both these quotations illustrate the main components of replacement theology; a casting away of national Israel and a replacing of them with a new entity – the Church. It is also important to hear it from those who hold to the view. Loraine Boettner writes:

"it may seem harsh to say that 'God is done with the Jews.' But the fact of the matter is that

He is through with them as a unified national group having anything more to do with the evangelization of the world. That mission has been taken from them and given to the Christian church" (Matt. 21:43).[3]

More recently it has become popular to use the term "fulfilment theology" in an attempt to distance itself from the negative connotations often associated with replacement theology. In this view all the Old Testament promises concerning Israel, the Land, and the future kingdom are seen to be completely fulfilled in Jesus Christ. This allows proponents to say they do not believe in traditional replacement theology, i.e. the Church has replaced Israel, because it is actually Christ who has replaced Israel by transferring the promises to Himself and we find a spiritual fulfilment of these promises in Him. Such language avoids the obvious redundancy that will be attributed to the party who have been "replaced", in preference for a softer, more nuanced motif of "fulfilment". Whatever the terminology being employed though, it soon becomes clear that the outcome is the same – Israel's unique calling and covenantal promises are taken from her and given to the Church. The often unspoken but logical consequence of such a belief is that there no longer remains any justification for her existence – a conclusion which, historically, has been catastrophic for the Jewish people.

Variations within Replacement Theology

To help us understand the issue further we can briefly outline the differences that exist between those who hold to a soft replacement idea and a more damaging hard replacement theology. Although there is broad agreement within replacement theology that national Israel has been supplanted by the Christian Church, and thus no longer maintains any unique covenantal status, the reasons given to support this can differ. The hard form focuses on Israel's disobedience and rebellion, seeing it as the catalyst for divine retribution and the primary cause for their rejection. Thus, the continued wickedness perpetrated by Israel in rebellion to God's divine commands means the nation has forfeited the right to be God's elect people and representatives on the earth. This overly negative view has fostered a deep-seated animosity towards the Jewish people in many of its adherents. Unfortunately, this view has found a home within segments of Christian theology. Church history is littered with statements that betray this attitude.

Origen.

The Church Father Origen (c. 185–254) commented:

"And we say with confidence that they will never be restored to their former condition. For they committed a crime of the most unhallowed kind, in conspiring against the Saviour of the human race in that city where they offered up to God a worship containing the symbols of mighty mysteries. It accordingly behoved that city where Jesus underwent these sufferings to perish utterly, and the Jewish nation to be overthrown, and the invitation to happiness offered them by God to pass to others – the Christians."[4]

The third century father Hippolytus of Rome wrote in his *Treatise Against the Jews:*

"Furthermore, hear this yet more serious word: "And their back do thou bend always;" that means, in order that they may be slaves to the nations, not four hundred and thirty years as in Egypt, nor seventy as in Babylon, but bend them to servitude, he says, "always."" [5]

Aside from the obvious theological concerns that are raised by such aggressive expressions of replacement theology, it is impossible to deny the strong anti-Judaic tones that accompany these doctrines. History is witness to the fact that these strong forms of replacement theology provide a fertile breeding ground for anti-Judaic activities, as we shall see later.

The softer forms of replacement theology do not attribute the replacement of the Jews to God's judgment on them for disobedience; they instead focus on the fact that Israel has served her purpose in the saga of redemption and thus no longer has a role. The place of Israel as the elect people of God was only ever intended to be temporary – it would expire with the arrival of the Messiah and the inauguration of the New Testament era.

The early Church Father Melito of Sardis gives us a clear expression of this teaching:

> "The people [Israel] were precious before the church arose, and the law was marvellous before the gospel was elucidated. But when the church arose and the gospel took precedence the model was made void, conceding its power to the reality... The people was made void when the church arose."[6]

It is easy to see how theologians who employ such language very easily make the leap from the "old Israel" being nothing more than a preliminary stage which will find its ultimate fulfilment in the "new Israel". The old Israel is associated with the Old Covenant and the new Israel formed with the commencement of the New Covenant. The Old Israel was a carnal entity consisting only of physical Israelites, while the new Israel has now been universalised into the Church. Such language, and the theological ideas behind it, will lead to one definite conclusion: The Jewish people and the nation of Israel represent a form of the kingdom which has been superseded by the Church and, therefore, Israel retains no special significance in the ongoing plan of redemption. Her role has been fulfilled. According to such theologians, to speak of "Israel" from a theological perspective, now means, the Church.

Many who hold to a softer form of replacement theology will be equally shocked at some of the content in this book and would have no hesitation or trouble repudiating it as completely antithetical to their Christian faith. On those matters we would agree. There have been many great theologians and preachers who see in the scriptures a teaching that the Church is either incorporated into an expanded Israel or is now in some way united with all believers into a 'spiritual Israel'. They would be able to affirm what New Testament scholar Dr. Darrell Bock points out, that the "inclusion of

Gentiles does not mean the exclusion of Israel."[7] However, whilst I would still differ with these soft forms of replacement theology, I acknowledge that many of these believers show a sincere love for the Jewish people and a desire for their salvation. Furthermore, I appreciate that they even believe in an eschatological revival amongst the Jews, and that their commitment to Jesus, the Jewish Messiah, would not allow them to support antisemitism in any form. Nevertheless, at the same time I am concerned that there often seems to be a sliding scale within replacement theology and, as we shall demonstrate, these beliefs can lead to the more aggressive, hard forms of replacement theology which are deeply concerning.

Ultimately, these are not neutral ideas; they have been actively believed and preached by many within the Church over the years, to different extents and with different motives. Yet time and again such attitudes have been accompanied by anti-Judaic sentiments and activity.

They make shrewd plans against *Your people*, and conspire together against Your treasured ones. They have said, "Come, and let us wipe them out as a nation, That the name of *Israel* be remembered no more."

Psalm 83:1-4

2

The History of Replacement Theology

The Apostolic Era (AD 33–100)

Initially the Church was viewed as a sect within Judaism, and no one today would really challenge the idea that Christianity in the beginning was made up almost exclusively of Jews. Given this, it is no surprise that they carried over many beliefs from the Judaism of their day. The Old Testament has a strong emphasis on the restoration of Israel in passages such as Jeremiah 31–33; Deuteronomy 30:1-10, Zechariah 14; and Ezekiel 36–37. This focus on the restoration of Israel was a core belief of Second Temple Judaism, although notions of restoration had been confused with political autonomy, a notion Jesus corrected during his earthly ministry. Yet we find the New Testament affirming the Old Testament expectation of restoration. In Luke 1:32-33 the angel Gabriel announces to Mary that "The Lord God will give Him the throne of His father David; and he will reign over the house of Jacob forever, and His kingdom will have no end". This seems to declare that

Jesus will one-day rule over the house of Israel (cf. Matthew 19:28).

Additional support for restorationism in the New Testament is found from Acts 1:6. In this verse we have the disciples' question to Jesus enquiring about the restoration of the Kingdom to Israel. Clearly the disciples still held nationalistic hopes concerning the Kingdom, even after 40 days of specific instruction by the resurrected Jesus of the "things concerning the Kingdom of God" (Acts 1:3). Restorationists have generally argued that although Jesus did refuse to address the timing of the kingdom, he did not take issue with the underlying premise of their question, nor did he see fit to correct them if they were mistaken. In addition, the promise of Paul in Romans 11:26-27 implies that the national salvation of Israel would coincide with the second coming. It seems that both the Old Testament and the New Testament explicitly affirm a future purpose for Israel. If this is the case, why all the controversy and how did this belief fare in subsequent eras of Church history?

The Patristic Era (AD 100–450)

The acceptance of replacement theology occurred early in the history of the Church. This seemed to go against the testimony of both the Old and New Testaments, indicating that other factors must have played a significant role in the Church's adoption of replacement doctrines. These doctrines were not formed in a vacuum but there were a number of events, both internal and external, that caused the development of this theology regarding Israel and the Church in the post-apostolic period. Scholars provide various lists of what they believe these circumstances were. These lists include issues ranging from the growing antagonism between Judaism and the messianic movement, to the increasing presence of antisemitism in the growing Gentile Church.

The Jewish revolts of AD 70 and AD 135 are often referred to as the beginning of "the parting of the way" and these marked a significant turning point for Jewish-Christian relations and for Judaism itself. With the Temple destroyed, disputes over how to perform Levitical rituals arose. Between

Arch of Titus Menorah. CC BY 3.0.

the two Jewish revolts a council was convened at the academy of *Yavneh* which began an intensive restructuring of Judaism. This marks the birth of rabbinical Judaism and during the years between the two revolts the relationship between Jews and Jewish Christians continued to deteriorate. Although this was a decisive turning point, it was the war of AD 132–135 that finally severed the two communities. Jewish Christians, unable to support the revolt due the messianic claims of its leader Bar Kokhba, were now considered traitors by their fellow Jews. A commitment to Bar Kokhba would have meant a denial of the Messiahship of Jesus.

The two remaining factors contributing to the development and acceptance of replacement theology are closely related. The increasing Gentile composition of the Church and the effect this had on biblical interpretation. One of the indirect consequences of the Bar-Kokhba rebellion was the issuing of a decree from the Roman leader Hadrian which forbade Jews from coming within sight of Jerusalem! This had huge ramifications for the Jerusalem Church. The early Church historian Eusebius tells us that, "down to the invasion of the Jews under Hadrian, there were fifteen bishops in that church, all which, they said, were Hebrews"[8]. After Hadrian's decree the Church had its first Gentile bishop – Marcus. This change led to the marginalizing of Jewish influence and importance.

As the Church was severed from the rich Jewish soil from which it was seeded, the methods the Church used to interpret the Bible also began to change. Gentile Christians who had no knowledge of Hebrew relied solely on the Greek Septuagint translation. These Gentile Christians brought with them Greek philosophical ideas, such as the allegorical methods of interpretation currently being popularised by the Alexandrian school.

This shift in the way the Bible was interpreted can be illustrated by looking at the major theologians of the period. An early example comes from the writings of Justin Martyr (AD 100–165) in the second century. In his work *Dialogue with Trypho*, a Jew, he argues for the first time in history that the Church is the true spiritual Israel:

> "For the true spiritual Israel, and descendants of Judah, Jacob, Isaac, and Abraham ... are we who have been led to God through this crucified Christ."[9]

Justin Martyr.

This set the precedent within early biblical interpretation for applying Old Testament promises made with Israel to the Church. A major figure to follow Justin was the theologian Origen of Alexandria (AD 185–254). He was a teacher at the school of Alexandria in Egypt at the beginning of the third century. It was under the influence of these teachers that the scriptures were harmonised with the beliefs of Greek philosophy. This naturally led to an allegorical approach being favoured over the more literalist approach of the early Jewish Church. Origen was really the first to formalise a system of interpretation that laid the foundation for the Church to spiritually appropriate the Old Testament promises made to Israel, by rooting allegory in biblical exegesis. This method was quickly adopted by the Church and became dominant throughout the Middle Ages.

Perhaps the most influential figure in Church history was the Bishop of Hippo, Augustine (AD 345–425). It was Augustine who took the system of interpretation of the early Church Fathers and systemised it into a comprehensive theology of 'last things' (eschatology) that would dominate Christianity for generations. The system of theology that Augustine left the Church is known as amillennialism. The amillennial view:

> "holds that the kingdom promises in the Old Testament are fulfilled spiritually rather than literally in the New Testament church."[10]

For three centuries before Augustine the Church had predominantly held *pre*millennial convictions. Based on a literal interpretation of the scriptures (notably Revelation

20:1-7), what is today called premillennialism envisaged that, following the appearance of the Antichrist, seven years of severe tribulation, and the catching away (rapture) of the saints, Christ's second coming (along with his saints) would usher in a *literal* golden-age of universal peace—which most understood to be 1,000 years. Esteemed Church Fathers like Irenaeus, Tertullian, Hippolytus, Polycarp and Justin Martyr were of this persuasion. However, the amillennial interpretation rejects a literal interpretation and, instead, utilizes the same allegorical methods of interpretation as the Alexandrian school. Practically, such a view empties the scriptures of any of their distinctive Jewish characteristics, as all promises made to a physical and ethnic Israel are now transferred to a spiritual and heavenly reality, known as the Church.

The dominance of Augustinian thought meant that, by the fifth century, the belief of the early Church in a literal restoration of the Jews to the Land of Israel had almost entirely disappeared. The replacement theology, inherent in the amillennial system, became the prevailing view of the Church until after the Reformation.

The Medieval Period (AD 450–1500)

The medieval Church was dominated by the acceptance of replacement theology, following after Augustine. In fact, right throughout the medieval era there was no real challenge to this view. As the ecclesiastical machine rose to power, Church and state become inseparably integrated. After the "conversion" of Emperor Constantine to Christianity in AD 313, Christianity became the religion of the Empire. The leader in Rome now acted as head over the Church and Christianity became nationalized. Over time, as ecclesiastical power became centralised in Rome, many were influenced to accept the Roman Catholic Church as, supposedly, the one true church on earth.

During the Middle Ages, the Catholic Church held incredible power over all the nations of Europe. This led to an appalling time of institutional antisemitism that planted deep roots into European culture. The Roman Church absorbed the antisemitism from the Greco-Roman world when their corrupted brand of Christianity became a state religion, and it added to this the theological antisemitism inherent in the replacement views of Augustine and his predecessors. Replacement theology was now the official view of the Church for the next one thousand years. The constant stream of formally sanctioned edicts and councils that were negative towards the Jewish people no doubt influenced the gross acts of physical antisemitism that surfaced throughout this period.

The negative stereotype of Jews during this period infiltrated every element of society. Clear evidence of this is carved in the rocks, printed in the news, passed through the laws, preached from the pulpits and painted on the canvases. The Jews were represented as monsters, nefarious creatures acting as agents of Satan in the world. Perhaps the most enduring symbol of anti-Jewish medieval Catholic replacement theology is the *Ecclesia* versus *Synagoga* imagery, which consists of two female statues: *Ecclesia* (the Church) is usually depicted standing at Christ's right hand, victorious and noble, with head held high and a crown on her head. She is usually holding a chalice and staff, representing her religious authority. *Synagoga* on the other hand is downcast, hunched over with a blindfold on. The benighted female is a clear slight against the Jews, as she loosely clings onto the tablets of the Law with one hand and has a broken staff in the other. Such statues can be found

Synagoga statue, By Immanuel Giel, CC BY-SA 4.0.

at Notre Dame in Paris and the Strasbourg Cathedral. This triumphalist imagery (the Gentile Church over the Jewish synagogue) is representative of the bad fruit that replacement theology produced throughout the Middle Ages.

Although the theological dialogue was not really advanced during this period, the repercussions of what had already been laid down came to the surface. As the medieval world gave us some of the most antisemitic atrocities in history. The inquisitions, the crusades, and the beginning of the blood libels, all of which had disastrous ramifications for the Jewish people, were from this period.

The Reformation Period (AD 1500–1700)

Although the reformers reacted strongly to the allegorical method of interpretation and rediscovered many great doctrinal truths such as justification by faith, they did not address the Augustinian legacy in matters relating to eschatology. This meant that their view regarding the restoration of Israel continued to be one of replacement. Although the great struggle of the Reformation was to break with the catholic-dominated ecclesiastical structure and place the authority back in the scriptures, unfortunately the underlying attitude towards the Jews was so entrenched that even the Reformation could not uproot it. The great reformer

Martin Luther was himself an Augustinian monk, a fact that no doubt influenced his understanding of Israel. Although initially seen to be favourable towards the Jews, when they did not respond to the gospel as he expected, the old stereotypes surfaced. His replacement theology views came out consistently in his preaching: the Jews had been rejected and the destruction of Jerusalem in AD 70 was evidence of this permanent rejection. In what is typical of replacement theology today, he also taught that Christians were now the true Israelites:

> "[T]he Jews are no longer Israel... Those alone are the true Israel who have accepted the new covenant..."[11]

Influenced as he was by Augustinian eschatology, Luther's replacement views surely contributed to his later antisemitism – unfortunately, this great reformer of the Church stands as a contender for producing the most antisemitic literature in history. Although other reformers such as John Calvin were more temperate in their denunciation of Israel, they still shared the anti-Jewish prejudices of the time, prejudices that undoubtedly had been honed through centuries of official Church teaching from a replacement perspective.

Another leading figure of the reformation, John Calvin,[12]

whose works are arguably more influential than even Luther's, also held derogatory views towards the Jews. Although scholars have rightly pointed out his comments are much more temperate when compared to Luther – should that really be the standard? Calvin held to the same Augustinian eschatology as Luther and often used overwhelmingly negative descriptions of the Jews in his writings. One incident, in reference to a disagreement with a rabbinical scholar, elicited the following comment from Calvin:

John Calvin.

"But here he not only betrays his ignorance, but his utter stupidity, since God so blinded the whole people that they were like restive dogs. I have had much conversation with many Jews – I have never seen either a drop of piety or a grain of truth or ingenuousness – nay, I have never found common sense in any Jew. But this fellow, who seems so sharp and ingenious, displays his own impudence to his great disgrace."[13]

It was not until the seventeenth century, among the English Puritans and the Dutch reformed Puritans, that a belief in the future conversion and restoration of the Jews began to return. This was based on a rejection of allegorical interpretation in the field of biblical prophecy.

The Modern Period (AD 1800–Present)

The last two centuries, more than any other period in the Church's history, witnessed a revival of interest in biblical prophecy and the Jewish people. The rise of fundamentalism within the evangelical Church led to a rejection of allegorical interpretations and a return to premillennialism. The growth of dispensationalism in the mid-nineteenth century fostered great interest and expectation in the restoration of the Jews. Dispensationalists emphasized a distinction between Israel and the Church and rejected any notion of replacement theology. They affirmed a future return of the Jews to the Land of Israel and a place of prominence for Israel during the coming millennial kingdom.

Dispensationalists also advocate a strong belief in the promises of Genesis 12:3, when God says to Abraham, "I will bless those who bless you, and the one who curses you I will curse". This has meant that generally there has been huge support for the Jewish people among dispensationalists. The popularity and influence of dispensational theology was accelerated across the

United States by men like Cyrus I. Scofield, who produced the popular Scofield reference Bible, and preachers like Dwight L. Moody. The rise of the Bible Conference movement along with a proliferation of books, Bible schools and teaching ministries led to a widespread acceptance of dispensational theology along with its strong emphasis on Israel and the Jews.

Two twentieth century events greatly impacted people's perceptions concerning Israel and the Jews. First, the tragic events of the Holocaust led to a period of soul-searching for Christendom. The tragic and premeditated murder of six million Jews at the hands of the Nazis is surely one of the greatest crimes in history. The second event was the re-establishment of the modern State of Israel to its ancient homeland (in 1948) after almost two thousand years. This event has divided opinion among theologians for many years. Many have been ready to embrace the newly formed state as a thrilling fulfilment of biblical

prophecy. Others argue that the modern State of Israel has no relevance to biblical prophecy at all, and they remain ambiguous as to modern Israel's role today. Still others see the establishment of the State of Israel as the mistaken creation of the Zionist enterprise.

The Shifting Face of Replacement Theology

This brief survey brings us up to the establishment of the State of Israel. Undoubtedly, much more could be said, but this will provide a framework to understand how the relationship between the Church and Israel has developed in the subsequent years. Although post-Holocaust theology brought about a welcome reappraisal of these beliefs, many scholars in recent years have noticed a resurgence of a new form of replacement theology that has been given fresh impetus by the conflict in the Middle East. The re-establishment of the State of Israel in 1948 has facilitated the presence of a robust and vigorous strand of Christian Zionism within the evangelical Church. This in turn has prompted the birth of a reactionary countermovement which is decisively anti-Zionist. This movement has been classified as 'Christian Palestinianism' and is the antithesis of Christian Zionism.

Christian Palestinianism takes traditional replacement doctrines and fuses them together with Palestinian liberation theology and an aggressive anti-Zionist narrative. Briefly, the Palestinian narrative focuses on the catastrophe of

1948, when Israeli troops, controlled by imperialist colonial powers, dispossessed indigenous Arabs from their ancient homeland called Palestine, which is now under Israeli occupation. This political narrative is largely what shapes the theology of Christian Palestinianism, which sees Israel as a 'racist state', guilty of 'apartheid', 'ethnic cleansing', and 'genocide'. This synthesis has given birth to a novel form of replacement theology, which has become known as 'the New Supersessionism'.

The New Supersessionism, and the narrative offered by Christian Palestinianism, has been gaining popularity in the western evangelical Church largely due to the efforts of a few high-profile evangelical Anglican scholars. Through a coordinated campaign of conferences, publications, documentaries, and social action they have successfully spread this anti-Israel narrative beyond the walls of the evangelical Church.

In the face of such a movement, the Church needs to ask itself a number of poignant and searching questions. Does this new form of replacement theology carry with it the risk of reviving this shameful legacy of Christian antisemitism? Can it even be soundly defended biblically? One social commentator suggests that the ancient doctrine of replacement theology, which had really only been supressed for a season after the Holocaust, has now "been revived under the influence of the Middle East conflict".[14] Canon Andrew White, a Church of

England Middle East representative, reasons:

> "... that Palestinian Christian revisionism has revived replacement theology. The catalyst for its re-emergence has been the attempt by Arab Christians to reinterpret the scripture in order to de-legitimize the Jews claim to the Land".[15]

White comments that this has already had an enormous effect upon the Church. Given these factors, the New Supersessionism constitutes a real challenge for Christian theology, if we are to ensure that we do not see a resurgence of antisemitism within the Christian Church. With such extreme anti-Israel sentiments being exchanged so freely among these segments of Christendom, and the documented link between replacement theology and antisemitic behaviour, we should be very concerned at the possibility that, as history has sadly proven, repeated verbal slanders might eventually bleed over into physical violence!

With such an overbearing political narrative informing the theological opinions of advocates of the New Supersessionism, can we really expect the biblical promises regarding the election of Israel and their national future to be taken at face value? With Israel being portrayed in such negative terms, hasn't the theological deck already been stacked?

I will make you a great *nation*, and I will bless you, and make your name *great*; and so you shall be a blessing; and I will bless those who bless you, and the one who curses you I will curse. And in you all the families of the earth will be *blessed*."

Genesis 12:2-3

3

Confronting the Past Theological Antisemitism

The following information is both hard to write yet at the same time necessary to read. Most Christians are to some extent aware of the atrocity called the Holocaust, even if few at the present time have ever studied the details. What is much less known is the long trail of antisemitism that preceded it. Throughout Western Europe especially, it comes as a big shock to evangelical ears when it is revealed just how complicit the mainstream churches were in this. The Jewish people have been subject to persecution, hatred, violence, murder, dispossessions, expulsions, libels, pogroms and mass extermination like no other ethnic or religious group. The hatred has known no bounds, has operated without borders, exploited every medium, and seemingly never dies.

One of the world's foremost authorities on antisemitism, the late Professor Robert Wistrich, who served as head of the Vidal Sassoon International Centre for Antisemitism at the

Hebrew University, researched this extensively. The cover synopsis for his seminal publication, *Anti-Semitism: The Longest Hatred*, reads as follows:

"No other prejudice has displayed such intensity and historic continuity, nor resulted in such devastating consequences, as anti-Semitism."[16]

Although a full study of worldwide antisemitism is beyond the scope of this book, there are many works that have undertaken such a task. Our focus shall instead be upon the theological antisemitism that flows naturally from the doctrines of replacement theology. As stated earlier, it would be misleading simply to imply that anyone who holds to replacement theology is automatically antisemitic, and it is true that there are many who, holding to the softer replacement views, still display a genuine love for the Jewish people and want to see them come to know the Lord.

Yet, the tragic history of the Church's relationship with the Jews proves that, very often, the opposite is true. The presence of Christian antisemitism has been called the "longest lasting Jew hatred in history".[17] Is it really possible to argue that hard replacement theology, with its clear theological belief that the Jews were cast aside due to their wickedness, is neutral in regard to Christian antisemitism? On the contrary, history is painfully clear that, when the Church adopted these triumphalist positions, it was predisposed to some of the most horrendous acts of antisemitism on record.

Christianity vs Christendom

The early Church had a turbulent existence for the first three centuries. Harsh persecutions under Roman emperors, from Nero (AD 54) to Diocletian (AD 245–313), ravaged much of the Christian population at those times. The status of Christianity was considered *religio illicita* (illegal religion), a situation which only changed under Constantine when he issued the Edict of Milan in AD 313, which gave freedom of worship to Christians. This edict changed the status of Christianity to a legal religion for the first time in the Empire. Although it was actually the Emperor Theodosius who declared Christianity to be the state religion in AD 380, the nationalisation of the faith had really begun with Constantine's edict. This changed status brought a needed respite from persecution for the Christian community, but it also led to new challenges. The centralisation of power under Constantine meant that ecclesiastical power now operated in unison with political power – an often-deadly mix.

Tragically, this union further diminished the already strained relationship between the Church and synagogue. The sudden influx of people confessing some sort of "Christian" faith multiplied exponentially. Now that the Emperor was a Christian it was acceptable for anyone to identify as a Christian; in fact, it was expedient to do so if one was seeking to improve their social status. In reality this meant that many people were now identifying as Christians in an external sense, regardless of whether they had a true saving faith in Christ, predicated upon biblical repentance.

Over time, as the Roman Church grew in its influence and its territorial expansion continued, entire nations and people groups began to identify as 'Christian'. Historically, territories in this situation were classified broadly as being part of 'Christendom' – a label that makes no real distinction between different groups sheltering under this banner.

Writing from the standpoint of evangelical Christianity, which emphasises the need for personal regeneration and saving faith, I would argue that much of what was labelled as "Christian" was nothing of the sort. In fact, much of it was (and is) antithetical to true Christianity. Practically this meant that the existing customs, and beliefs of the nations, often were simply overlaid with a verbal acceptance of Christianity – or later, an allegiance to the Papal authorities. Often, the existing negative attitudes towards the Jews of the ancient world were absorbed into the 'Church' through this unfortunate conflation of the Church with 'Christendom'. This is not the biblical definition of the Church, which is solely comprised of people who have been "born again" (John 3:16) and who, in that way, have become part of the true, universal Church, the Body of Christ (1 Corinthians 12:12-13). Unfortunately, for those predisposed to anti-Judaic sentiments, the teachings of replacement theology were seen as providing adequate justification for them to continue with their prejudices under the banner of this nationalised form of 'Christianity'.

Now that the official Church decided the law, it held political power; thus theological antisemitism could be institutionalised in cannon law. This happened almost overnight. The first great Ecumenical Council of the Church was convened by the Emperor Constantine in AD 325.

The Council of Nicaea – Setting the Stage

Many Christians are aware of the Council of Nicaea and its valiant attempts at defending the nature of Christ against the heretical Arians who denied his deity (arguing that the Son of God was created by the Father). Traditional churches still recite the Nicene Creed. How tragic it is, then, that the same council set the precedent for passing anti-Jewish laws and effectively institutionalised antisemitism within the Church.

The most significant piece of legislation passed at this council relating to Jewish-Christian relations was the ruling that separated Passover and Easter. The rationale that Constantine gives, as we read it today, is dripping with anti-

The Council of Nicea, Fresco in the Sistine Salon Vatican.

Jewish sentiment. He stated that it is an unworthy thing to "follow the practice of the Jews, who have impiously defiled their hands with enormous sin, and are, therefore, deservedly afflicted with blindness of soul". He continues, "Let us then have nothing in common with the detestable Jewish crowd". He also put the charge of deicide ('killing God') into the statute books – a charge that has been used by almost every anti-Semite since. He states:

> "For how should they be capable of forming a sound judgment, who, since their parricidal guilt [the guilt of 'killing a parent'] in slaying their Lord, have been subject to the direction, not of reason, but of ungoverned passion, and are swayed by every impulse of the mad spirit that is in them?"[18]

Coming from the 'Christian' Emperor it is easy to see how this influenced people's perceptions of the Jews at this time. The anti-Jewish rhetoric included at the Council of Nicaea gave the green light for future councils to further build upon that contemptible foundation by formulating their own antisemitic laws and decrees. Indeed, after that time it became common place for the Church to legislate against the Jews.

In AD 341 the council of Antioch enforced the decree concerning Easter and Passover by threatening any Christian who celebrated Passover with excommunication. At the synod of Laodicea in AD 364 Christians were forbidden from resting on the sabbath day because this would be to judaize. It was also decreed that Christians could not celebrate any holiday along with the Jews, nor partake of unleavened bread during Passover.[19] In Vannes (AD 465) Christians were prohibited from sharing meals with Jews, and from marrying Jews in the council of Chalcedon (AD 451) and the second council of Orleans (AD 533). At the third council of Orleans (AD 538) harsh social restrictions were enacted, prohibiting Jews from acting as Judges and from appearing in public between Maundy Thursday and Easter Monday.

Constantine statue, York.
By Chabe01, CC BY-SA 4.0.

The Toledo Councils

Eleven hundred years later, in the seventeenth century, a number of ecclesiastical councils were held in the city of Toledo, Spain. These councils had "the radical goal of seeking to uproot Judaism entirely".[20] At this time the Catholic Church was attempting to 'Christianise' the whole of Spain. Over the course of approximately a century these councils further denigrated the Jews among them. At Toledo III it was decreed that children born to a mixed marriage of a Jew and a Christian had to be baptized as Christians. Also, Jews were not permitted to hold public office. This became even worse at Toledo IV which forbade "converted" Jews from returning to Judaism. Mixed marriages were now forcibly dissolved and the ban on Jews holding public office was applied to their descendants too.

Toledo VI "confirmed the expulsion from the country of the persistent Jews and ordered those already converted to make public confession of their adherence to Christianity". And as a final insult the Toledo XVII council practically reduced to the status of slaves any Jews who were found to be practicing Judaism in the Visigoth Kingdom of Spain. Their children were taken from them and placed into 'Christian' homes where they could be raised in the faith. Finally, any property that was owned by Jews was forcibly confiscated.[21] Such harsh laws made living under 'Christian rule' a demeaning and dangerous existence. There were many forced conversions during this period, leading up to the infamous Spanish Inquisition a little later. Usually, new Jewish 'converts' were required to publicly renounce all things Jewish. The following is a sampling of one such confession of faith from the Church of Constantinople:

> "[A] Jew must confess and denounce verbally the whole Hebrew people, and forthwith declare that with a whole heart and sincere faith he desires to be received among the Christians. Then he must renounce openly in the church all Jewish superstition, the priest saying, and he, or his sponsor if he is a child, replying in these words: 'I renounce all customs, rites, legalisms, unleavened breads and sacrifices of lambs of the Hebrews, and all the other feasts of the Hebrews, sacrifices, prayers, aspersions, purifications, sanctifications and propitiations, and fasts, and new moons, and Sabbaths, and superstitions, and hymns and chants and observances and synagogues, and the food and drink of the Hebrews; in one word, I renounce absolutely everything Jewish, every law, rite and custom..."[22]

Imperial Codes

It was not just the ecclesiastical bodies who were making harsh, anti-Jewish legislation through this period. The Emperors were also issuing imperial codes that followed closely the same approach taken by the Church – as the two were very much aligned at this stage in history. These imperial codes are clearly borne of the same replacement theology perspective that influenced the Church. Now, government laws, not just ecclesiastical laws, were influenced by the corrosive effects of replacement theology.

The two most relevant early codes were the Theodosian Code and the Justinian Code. The first, produced by Theodosius II, was a compilation of laws from the time of Constantine until its completion in AD 438. Although there was a measure of protection for Judaism built into this code, it still prohibited Jews from certain professions and from attending many public functions. The same derogatory language that was common at that time is still sometimes used today. Judaism is described as "a wicked sect" and Jews themselves as "abominable".[23] The second, extremely influential, code is the Justinian Code, compiled in two versions during the reign of Emperor Justinian (527–565). It was designed to bring together all the previous statements from the Theodosian Code, remove any that were no longer relevant and update the Code where necessary. The Justinian Code was influential in the West for many centuries afterwards, and its preservation is how we know so much about Roman law. The Justinian Code contained the same Jewish restrictions found in the earlier codes but was also responsible for further restrictions. In 531, Justinian ruled that heretics and Jews could not give testimony in court against orthodox Christians. The most debated novel law of Justinian was the one relating to what could or could not be read in the synagogues. Whilst Hebrew and Greek were deemed acceptable, the Law specifically forbade something called *deuterosis*. This reference comes when discussing the languages used in the synagogue:

> "What they call Mishnah (= *deuterosis*), on the other hand, we prohibit entirely, for it is not included among the Holy Books, nor was it handed down from above by the prophets, but is an invention of men in their chatter, exclusively of earthly origin and having in it nothing of the divine. Let them read the Holy words themselves, therefore, in unfolding these Holy books for reading, but without hiding what is said in them, on the one hand, and without accepting extraneous and unwritten nonsense they themselves had contrived to the perdition of the more simple minded, on the other hand."[24]

Most people presume that what is being referred to is the reading of the oral law in conjunction with the Scripture reading in the synagogue. It is really part of the ongoing debate about Jewish-Christian interpretation of the Bible. It seems that, by banning the Mishnah, they hoped the Jews would come to see the scriptures in the same way as the Christians. Whether this was enforced is hard to tell but the fact that it was enshrined into an imperial law code was probably designed as a polemic to demonstrate the superiority of Christianity over Judaism.

Literature of the Church

In the centuries that followed the apostolic period, the early Church developed an *Adversos Judaeos* (literally, 'against the Jews') tradition that consisted of a growing collection of polemical works aimed at the Jews themselves. The selection below is only a meagre sample of what can be found. In the second century the Church Father Hippolytus (AD 160–235) wrote a volume called "*Expository Treatise against the Jews*" in which he called the Jewish people a perverse race, guilty of deicide and justly suffering for all they had done, thus rightly condemned to perpetual slavery. In the mid third century, Cyprian, Bishop of Carthage, wrote a three-volume tome called "*Testimonies against the Jews*", making the familiar charge of deicide. He clearly stated that Jesus "was put to death by the Jews". It is very clear that he held to the reigning replacement view, when we read his statement that "the gentiles rather than the Jews will inherit the Kingdom".[25] Father Aphrahat, a Syrian Church Father, in a volume called *"Demonstrations against the Jews"*, equated Jerusalem with Sodom and Gomorrah. He stated that "they [the Jews] that crucified Him shall be burned in flames at the end", and furthermore, "Israel has played the whore, and Judah has committed adultery. And the people which is of [the Christian Church] is the holy and faithful people, which has gone down and adhered to the Lord".[26] Eighth century Greek Orthodox priest John of Damascene wrote in *"Against the Jews on the Sabbath Question"*, that God gave the Sabbath, "knowing the denseness of the Israelites and their carnal love and propensity towards matter in everything".[27]

The Bishop of Constantinople, John Chrysostom (AD 345–405), known as the golden mouth preacher, preached a series of sermons entitled *"Orations against the Jews"*. These attacked the Jewish people with such vehemence that they are some of the most antisemitic writings on record. To him, the synagogue was a "whorehouse" and "a den of thieves", "a temple of demons"; the Jews are "no better than pigs and goats in their lewd grossness", they are also "lustful, rapacious, greedy, perfidious, bandits ... inveterate murderers, men possessed by the devil". Finally, Chrysostom declared that "God has always hated the Jews, [and] it is incumbent upon all Christians to hate the Jews".[28] Reiterating such statements makes shocking reading for modern Christians, coming as these statements do from such renowned teachers of the Patristic period, but any honest reading of the history of antisemitism would otherwise be woefully incomplete.

The most influential Church Father, whose works would enjoy near canonical status in the medieval Church, and exerted considerable influence on Reformation thinkers too, is Augustine of Hippo (AD 354–430). Although Augustine's attitude towards the Jews was less severe in its language than Chrysostom, it nonetheless has been influential throughout Church history. Augustine was reluctant to opt for a hard

St. Augustine by Carlo Crivelli.

replacement view that would reject any ongoing purpose for Israel, rather he formulated what has come to be known as his 'witness doctrine'. Based on his exposition of Psalm 59, Augustine came up with a solution that would in some measure maintain a rationale for Israel's continued existence, while also denying them any significant role in the Kingdom, as he interpreted its current form. Augustine comments on Psalm 59:11, which reads "Do not slay them, or my people will forget", that it may be understood as speaking about the Jews:

> "This indeed may be also understood of the Jews… The Jews nevertheless remain with a mark; nor in such sort conquered have they been, as that by the conquerors they have been swallowed up. Not without reason is there that Cain, on whom, when he had slain his brother, God set a mark in order that no one should slay him, Genesis 4:15. This is the mark which the Jews have: they hold fast by the remnant of their law, they are circumcised, they keep Sabbaths, they sacrifice the Passover; they eat unleavened bread. These are therefore Jews, they have not been slain, they are necessary to believing nations. Why so? In order that He may show to us among our enemies His mercy."[29]

Then on the second part of the verse Augustine comments:

> " "Scatter them abroad in Your virtue" Now this thing has been done: throughout all nations there have been scattered abroad the Jews, witnesses of their own iniquity and our truth... take away from them virtue, take away from them their strength."[30]

Tragically, such a degrading view of the Jews, whereby their only purpose is to be left on the earth as wanderers, a witness to the fate of those who reject Christ, has led to many centuries of shameful anti-Judaic treatment throughout history and has contributed to the stereotype of the wandering Jew.

The Cappadocian Father, St. Gregory of Nyssa (331–396) describes the Jews as:

> "slayers of the Lord, murderers of the prophets, enemies and haters of God, adversaries of grace, enemies of their fathers' faith, advocates of the devil, a brood of vipers, slanderers, scoffers, men of darkened minds, the leaven of Pharisees, a congregation of demons, sinners, wicked men, haters of goodness!"[31]

The following centuries were marked by numerous vicious blood libels, the demonising of the Jews and institutionalised antisemitism. This vicious pattern continued all through the medieval period.

The Reformation leader Martin Luther was initially quite favourable towards the Jews, but this changed after his hope of seeing them accept the Gospel failed to be realised. He continued the *Adversus Judaeos* tradition with his 1542 tract *"On the Jews and their Lies"*, which someone has described as the "blueprint for modern anti-Semitic literature".[32] Wistrich calls it a work "of medieval hatred which contains some of the most violent language in the history of anti-Semitism".[33] The hateful language used against the Jews is second to none in Church history. He recycles virtually every antisemitic stereotype possible, the Jews are "a plague, a pestilence", "idle and lazy", "murderers", "the vilest whores and rogues under the sun" and the "devil's children". He libels them for poisoning wells and engaging in the ritual murder of Christian children, and he recommended that they should be "hanged on the gallows seven times higher than other thieves". Such statements are shocking enough, coming from a man revered by much of the Christian Church, but his seven-points of "sharp mercy" – a 'solution' of what to do with the Jews – is perhaps the highest pinnacle of Christian antisemitic literature. It is reproduced at length below for your thoughtful contemplation:[34]

"Firstly, to set fire to their synagogues or schools and to bury and cover with dirt whatever will not burn, so that no man will ever again see a stone or cinder of them.

Secondly, I advise that their houses also be razed and destroyed. For they pursue in them the same aims as in their synagogues. Instead, they might be lodged under a roof or a barn, like the gypsies. This will bring home to them the fact that they are not masters in our country.

Thirdly, they should be deprived of their prayer books and Talmud's in which such idolatry, lies, cursing and blasphemy are taught.

Fourthly, their Rabbis must be forbidden under threat of death to teach any more...

Fifthly, I advise safe-conduct on highways be abolished completely for the Jews.

Sixthly, I advise that usury be prohibited to them, and that all cash and treasure of silver and gold be taken from them and put aside for safekeeping.

Seventh, I recommend putting a fail, an axe, a hoe, a spade ... into the hands of young, strong Jews and let them earn their bread by the sweat of their brow."[35]

Such direct and chilling statements coming from the pen of one of the greatest Christian reformers should give us all pause for thought. Is it really any wonder that we find Luther's works being used by the Nazis in defence of their atrocities at the Nuremburg War Crimes Tribunal? As we shall now see, such viewpoints never stay on the written page, they are never just theorising – it is almost inevitable, indeed predictable, that, at some point theory will become practice.

Libels and Massacres

The tragic legacy of this institutionalised antisemitism is visible throughout history. It constitutes one of the dark shadows that hangs over this fallen world and one that should drive the Church to repentance and a determination to expunge even the roots of such attitudes from our thinking. The historian Paul Johnson, in his massive work *A History of the Jews*, gives us this message:

> "One of the principal lessons of Jewish history has been that repeated verbal slanders are sooner or later followed by violent physical deeds. Time and again over the centuries, antisemitic writings created their own fearful momentum which climaxed in an effusion of Jewish blood."[36]

Without a doubt the medieval period for Jews, particularly in western Europe, was one of the worst periods of history. It is from that period that we see the emergence of many of the antisemitic patterns that were to follow for centuries afterwards. The authority of the Catholic Church over western nations, its institutionalised doctrines of replacement theology, and its command of state and imperial armies had become a serious threat to the Jews.

The Crusades

The year 1096 is seared into the collective Jewish consciousness of the medieval period, the year of the First Crusade under the summons of Pope Urban II. Although the Crusades were primarily a response to Muslim aggression in the Holy Land, what transpired in many cases was that bands of mercenaries, fired up by the antisemitic preaching of men like Peter the Hermit and his associate Walter Sansavoir,[37] took the opportunity to fight against all "enemies of God". The Jewish communities that happened to be in the path of these soldiers often suffered brutally, usually being given the option of baptism or death. All along the Rhine Valley, and into Northern France, Jewish communities were massacred. Although efforts were made to shield the Jews by certain Bishops and others, the might of the Crusaders usually prevailed. In only six months it is estimated that over 10,000 Jews were murdered. The vilest display occurred in Jerusalem in 1099. The Jews were rounded up and locked inside a synagogue which was then set on fire. The Crusaders then watched the gruesome spectacle as they sang the hymn "Christ, We Adore You. I cannot think of an action that is more antithetical to the heart of the Jewish Messiah and true Christian faith.

PETER THE HERMIT PREACHING THE FIRST CRUSADE.

Blood Libels

The Jews have always been used as scapegoats and there is none that historically was more persistent than the charge of "blood libel". This was an accusation that the Jews had officially murdered a Christian child in a ritual sacrifice – usually during Holy Week in order to use the blood in their Passover ceremony. If you have never heard of this before you would be forgiven for thinking the charge is so far-fetched as to be ridiculous. However, libels like this were dyed deep into the fabric of European Christendom during the Middle Ages, and tragically still exist today in their modern equivalents.

Although one can find libels used against the Jews in antiquity by the Greeks and Romans, the first recorded libel in the early medieval era is recorded in England in the twelfth century. In Norwich, 1141, a body of a boy was found on Good Friday and, on the basis of dubious testimony, it was claimed that the Jews plan a yearly murder to insult the death of Christ, and this unfortunate boy was a victim of the Jews. Similar charges started to become a recurring theme in England and throughout Europe.

There were libels involving so-called "host desecration", the theft of consecrated Eucharist wafers by Jews so that, allegedly, they could pierce them through to insult the body of Christ.[38] When such accusations arose in Belitz, Germany, all the Jews of the town were burned. Over a hundred instances of this accusation have been recorded.[39] Since that time it became acceptable to use the Jews as a scapegoat for any calamity. It is widely accepted that, when King's treasuries were running a little low, a libel would appear, Jewish-owned property would be seized, and Jewish populations forced to pay extra taxes. Whether it was blaming the Jews for global plots to dominate the world, or for the onset of a plague, for the next several centuries libels became an all-too-familiar feature of Jewish existence and were responsible for the loss of thousands of Jewish lives.

Sadly, antisemitic blood libel accusations still sometimes appear in the state-sponsored media of some Arab and Islamic nations.[40]

The Modern Revision

With the influence of the Reformation in the sixteenth century and the Enlightenment of the eighteenth century many new ideals emerged. The marriage between Church and state was broken, as was the influence of religion in many areas. This meant that the ever-adaptable scourge of antisemitism shifted to fit the new era. Religious antisemitism now morphed into a new racial antisemitism. The enlightenment dismissed the role of religion and elevated the place of rationality and science. Therefore, the Jew haters could not as easily get away with using loaded religious terminology and imagery as they had in times gone by.

With the emergence of Darwinian evolutionary theory, the concept of different human 'races' inexorably influenced and, in some cases, began replacing, the religious structures used to view the world. It was not long before scientists were proposing theories of 'lower' and 'higher' races. For many famous enlightenment thinkers, the Jewish race was an example of an inferior race. From the late nineteenth century onwards, policies in nations of the ostensibly civilised West began advocating (and in many cases enforcing) so-called 'racial hygiene' and radical eugenics – the harbinger of truly horrific actions of the twentieth century. Of course, this sort of pseudo-scientific racial antisemitism came to fruition during the rule of Nazi Germany. In the end such language was just another manifestation of the age-old hatred of the Jews.

After the horrors of the Holocaust the world was shocked into accepting the reality of exterminatory antisemitism. This collective guilt led to a number of measures in both the theological and secular worlds to ensure that such atrocities could never happen again. For one thing, racial hygiene and eugenics were immediately execrated. The traditional language of antisemitism was pushed to the fringes of society and acceptable discourse. However, this does not mean that antisemitism disappeared – the sinfulness of people's hearts meant that it just had to be refashioned and reinvented once again.

What I am saying is this: the Law, which came four hundred and thirty years later, does not invalidate a *covenant* previously ratified by God, so as to nullify the promise.

Galatians 3:17

4

The New Antisemitism & the New Replacement Theology

Modern Revisions of Old Teachings

Earlier I mentioned that replacement theology had changed its face in recent times into a liberationist movement known as Christian Palestinianism. The question was raised as to whether this new movement runs the risk of reviving a similar legacy of theological antisemitism that was present in the past. The risk is very real and to understand it we need to examine the way antisemitism has been substituted for the term anti-Zionism (being against the State of Israel).

Antisemitism, as we have seen, is like a virus that mutates with the ever-changing cultural zeitgeist, always there, bubbling under the surface and waiting for the right time to rear its ugly head. Britain's ex-chief Rabbi Jonathan Sacks comments that:

"In the Middle Ages, Jews were hated because of their religion. In the 19th and 20th centuries they were hated because of their race. Today they are hated because of their nation state, Israel. Anti-Zionism is the new anti-Semitism."[41]

A new working definition of antisemitism by the *International Holocaust Remembrance Alliance* states:

"Antisemitism is a certain perception of Jews, which may be expressed as hatred toward Jews. Rhetorical and physical manifestations of antisemitism are directed toward Jewish or non-Jewish individuals and/or their property, toward Jewish community institutions and religious facilities."

This is followed by a number of examples to help guide the use of the definition:

"Manifestations might include the targeting of the state of Israel, conceived as a Jewish collective.

Denying the Jewish people their right to self-determination, e.g., by claiming that the existence of a State of Israel is a racist endeavour. Drawing comparisons of contemporary Israeli policy to that of the Nazis."[42]

These statements add to the growing chorus of leaders and organisations that have come to recognize the growing ideological threat. Much of what is being done under the banner of anti-Zionism is barely distinguishable from classical antisemitism, except that it has been rebranded, given new terminology, and as Phyllis Chesler points out, ironically "is now being perpetrated in the name of anti-racism and anti-colonialism by supposed politically correct human rights activists."[43]

This new ideological facelift had provided a measure of respectability to the anti-Zionist cause. In the mind of its advocates, if the State of Israel can be likened to an evil oppressor then any attempt to "free the oppressed" cannot be racism, rather it is an issue of "human rights". This narrative plays right into the hands of the liberation theologians who have combined it with their theological replacement views. With this skewed perception of reality, attacking the Jewish state collectively is not perceived to be the same as attacking Jews individually. Pushing for the boycott of Israeli businesses and academics is not considered the same as the Third Reich boycotting Jewish owned businesses because, supposedly, this is now done with noble motivations – a desire to speak up for the oppressed. However, behind the curtain of such word games and political manoeuvring, it is becoming increasingly obvious to many onlookers that anti-Zionism is nothing more than an ideopolitical project, one whose ultimate aim is the destruction of the State of Israel, the "removal of the Zionist entity". In this sense, anti-Zionism is really no different from its ideological forbear and should rightly be labelled antisemitic.

Of course, many will protest vigorously that they are simply anti-Zionist and only disagree with the policies of the Israeli government, that they are not in any way antisemitic, so it is wrong to equate the two. While it is true that the two are not identical, often they do morph into one and the same, becoming virtually indistinguishable in the minds of many people. A valid, albeit negative, criticism of Israeli policy should not be considered antisemitic. In reality, I do not think anyone is being labelled antisemitic just for criticising Israeli policy; in fact, democracies welcome criticism since they act as a catalyst for positive change. However, questions are raised when condemnations of Israel cross the line from being valid criticisms to forms of denigration that could be rightly classed as antisemitic, "since this new antisemitism can hide behind the veneer of legitimate criticism of Israel".[44]

To help expose this new antisemitism it is helpful to know why the term anti-Zionism emerged in the first place. Historian Paul Johnson traces its modern usage back to the Cold War period. He notes that, in the period following WWII, the Soviet campaign against the Jews was "conducted under the codename of anti-Zionism, which became a cover for every variety of anti-Semitism".[45] From the early 1950s, the Soviet anti-Zionist propaganda stressed the links between Zionism, the Jews in general, and Judaism. Johnson comments that the fact that "Zionism in practice stood for 'the Jews' became quickly apparent".[46]

Similarly, Professor Dan Cohn-Sherbok, in his volume *Anti-Semitism* (2009), explains that during the 1970's the left-wing media created new themes to manipulate public opinion. Zionism was equated with racism and even Nazism, and Israel was seen as a terror-state, seeking the genocide of the Palestinians. He concludes, "here then is a new form of Judaeo-phobia, political in character yet rooted in inherited stereotypical images from the past".[47]

Former minister Nathan Sharansky, who as a dissident in the former Soviet Union monitored antisemitism, laid out the criteria for distinguishing these boundaries in his article, "Anti-Semitism in 3D".[48] The 3D's of the new antisemitism are demonization, double standards and delegitimisation.

Unfortunately, it is possible to find examples of all three D's in the writings and actions of the anti-Zionist movements. Tragically, it is pertinent to note that this particularly includes the writings coming from the Christian academics who advocate the new form of replacement theology. Their accusations of racism and apartheid, along with Nazi comparisons, serve to both demonise and delegitimise the State of Israel. The fact that such rhetoric has found its way into Christian circles should be a cause of great concern for Christians of all theological persuasions. Perhaps the most noticeable element of the new replacement theology is the double standard; a very one-sided approach is being used to criticise Israel. To speak of supposed Israeli "apartheid" whilst simultaneously ignoring the well documented gender, sexual, and religious apartheid existing throughout the Middle East is to apply a double standard. To condemn Israel as one of the chief human rights violators in the world without condemning the rampant human rights violations by surrounding nations is a double standard.[49]

It is for these reasons that the world is slowly waking up to the fact that anti-Zionism, although politically focused, still resembles classical antisemitism. Again, there is nothing wrong with bringing forward legitimate criticism about the State of Israel, but where this criticism involves an attempt to demonise and delegitimise the State of Israel by applying double standards then this may properly be identified as The

New Antisemitism. When this is done under the guise of Christian theology the ramifications are even more serious – history has proven that, when the Church gives theological justification for antisemitism, Jewish bloodshed often follows. The heart of our Lord Jesus, himself a Jew, must weep once again for His people.

Seeing with Spiritual Eyes

As Christians we unequivocally denounce all forms of racism. At its core, racism is a fundamental denial of the equality that all humans share because we are made in the image of God. Yet, at the same time, there seems to be something unique about Jew-hatred, given its longevity, ferocity and ability to cross all cultural, political and religious boundaries. Ultimately, there is no reasonable, 'natural' explanation for why this is the case – it lies in the spiritual realm. As Christians we need to examine the world through the lens of scripture. We need to apply a biblical worldview to all areas of life – the issue of antisemitism included.

Scripture shows us that the onslaught we see against the Jews is driven behind the scenes by a supernatural enemy – Satan. The apostle John pulls back the spiritual curtain for us and provides a panoramic view of world history seen from the perspective of Jewish persecution:

A great sign appeared in heaven: a woman clothed with the sun, and the moon under her feet, and on her head a crown of twelve stars; and she was with child; and she cried out, being in labor and in pain to give birth. Then another sign appeared in heaven: and behold, a great red dragon having seven heads and ten horns, and on his heads were seven diadems. And his tail swept away a third of the stars of heaven and threw them to the earth. And the dragon stood before the woman who was about to give birth, so that when she gave birth he might devour her child. And she gave birth to a son, a male child, who is to rule all the nations with a rod of iron; and her child was caught up to God and to His throne. Then the woman fled into the wilderness where she had a place prepared by God, so that there she would be nourished for one thousand two hundred and sixty days.

Revelation 12:1-6

Although the language is unusual because it is written using the symbols and imagery common to the apocalyptic genre, it can still be understood from the context. The Bible is its own best interpreter and the symbols are explained elsewhere in the text. The fact that this genre uses symbols does not take away from the real historical truth that it seeks to convey. In this text we are given two signs in the heavens. The first is "the woman", identified as Israel from the imagery of the sun, moon and stars taken from Joseph's dream back in Genesis 37:9-11. This woman is said to be pregnant.

The second sign is "the great red dragon", a clear reference to Satan (Revelation 12:9). The dragon is pictured as standing before the woman, waiting to devour the child. The woman gave "birth to a son" – the Messiah, who will rule the nations. Here we see the angelic conflict that lies behind the satanic attempts to destroy Israel and her Messiah. Satan hates Israel because she is the vehicle through whom the Messiah came into the world. This is building upon the narrative in Genesis that the seed of the woman will defeat the seed of the serpent (Genesis 3:15). Israel testifies to the veracity of God's promises that this Son will rule but Satan will not. Therefore, Satan will try everything in his power to remove this divine testimony from the earth and stop the child from ruling. This, ultimately, is the spiritual battle that manifests itself in the antisemitism which has plagued the Jews' long history.

The promises in Scripture that relate to the "child" of Revelation 12 are contained within the covenants that God made with the people of Israel (Romans 9:5). Chiefly, these are: the Abrahamic covenant (Genesis 12:1-3; 15:18-21), the Davidic covenant (2 Samuel 7:8-14) and the New covenant (Jeremiah 31:31-34). These together contain God's promises to bless the children of Israel with both a Land and a Royal seed (the Son), who would go on to bless the entire world with the forgiveness of sins, as well as rule with a rod of iron. These covenants contain the promises of God, which represent His character and nature, and these covenants were given to the house of Israel.

This connection explains why such disproportionate hatred (considering the actual Jewish population size) is directed toward the Jews: it is the outworking of the spiritual conflict in the heavenlies that we have just peered into through John the apostle's apocalyptic vision (Revelation 12). The Jews were and continue to be God's covenant people to this day (Romans 11:1). These covenants affirm the enduring place and purpose for Israel in God's redemptive kingdom program, even while they are in a state of unbelief (Romans 11:25). Much is at stake here: the satanic onslaught against the Jewish people actually reflects the attempt by Satan to discredit God by showing that His promises can be broken! Satan is the "prince of the power of the air" (Ephesians 2:2) and the "god of this world" (2 Corinthians 4:4) and he does his utmost to mobilize the masses in pursuit of his goal. Such devilish ambitions are expressed by the ancient enemies of Israel in Psalm 83, and similar sentiments could be listed from world leaders today:

> They make shrewd plans against Your people, and conspire together against Your treasured ones. They have said, 'Come, and let us wipe them out as a nation, that the name of Israel be remembered no more.'
>
> **Psalm 83:3-4**

Antiochus coin - By Classical Numismatic Group, CC BY-SA 3.0.

Satan has tried to wipe out the Jews many times in history. In the Bible we see the Egyptian Pharaoh ordering the Midwives to kill all the Jewish children. During the Persian Empire we see a man called Haman attempting to manipulate the throne in order to eradicate the Jewish Population. Then we learn of the Greek King, Antiochus Epiphanes, whose hatred of the Jews and desecration of the Jewish Temple led to the Maccabean rebellion. Satanically inspired attempts to eradicate the Jews continue in the New Testament. For instance, we see Herod destroy the Jewish children for fear that one of them was the promised King.

Nationally, the Bible shows us the Egyptians, the Amalekites, the Babylonians, the Hittites, the Assyrians, and the Romans have all persecuted the nation of Israel. This satanic attempt is clearly witnessed in modern times with the racial antisemitism of the Third Reich, the devastating Russian Pogroms, and the ongoing Islamic antisemitism rampant across parts of the globe.

Yet despite this, we can have full assurance that Satan will never succeed. In Jeremiah 31 God says:

> Thus says the Lord, who gives the sun for light by day and the fixed order of the moon and the stars for light by night, who stirs up the sea so that its waves roar; The Lord of hosts is His name: "If this fixed order departs from before Me," declares the Lord, "Then the offspring of Israel also will cease from being a nation before Me forever." Thus says the Lord, "If the heavens above can be measured and the foundations of the earth searched out below, then I will also cast off all the offspring of Israel for all that they have done," declares the Lord. Jeremiah 31:35-37

In other words, it is impossible because the existence of the Jewish people is a testimony to God's enduring faithfulness to keep His promises.

You worship what you do not know; we *worship* what we know, for salvation is from the Jews.

John 4:22

5

Bible Verses used to Support Replacement Theology

One of the main arguments of replacement theology is that the Church is the new Israel or is now spiritual Israel, but such a bold claim requires scriptural justification. In this section we shall examine some of the scriptures that replacement theologians have used to justify this assertion. The word Israel is used a total of seventy-three times in the New Testament. In nearly all cases there is no doubt that it refers to ethnic Israel. However, replacement theologians make a lot of the one or two places where a measure of ambiguity exists. The most frequently used texts will be examined below.

Galatians 6:16

> And those who will walk by this rule, peace and mercy be upon them, and upon the Israel of God.

This text, above all others, is put forward by replacement theologians as definitively stating that the Church is called Israel in the bible. Their argument revolves around the correct meaning of the Greek word *kai* ("and") just before the phrase "Israel of God". They argue that this connecting particle should be translated to give the sense of "even" or be omitted.[50] This would then mean that the text is only referring to one group of people and not two. There are "those who walk by this rule" – obviously referring to Gentile Christians in the Church – but replacement theologians insist they are then referred to by another name, "the Israel of God". From their point of view, this is clear evidence that the Church is now referred to as the new Israel, therefore this can now be used as justification for their entire system.

There are a number of reasons why this interpretation should be reconsidered. A much stronger case can be made that Paul is referring to two distinct groups in his statement. The phrase "Israel of God" is being used as a designation for Jewish believers within the Church and not as a blanket designation for the Church in general.

Firstly, the replacement theologian's exegetical basis for translating *kai* (and) as "even" is weak. Although technically the Greek word can be translated in this way it is a much rarer grammatical form. It is unusual to opt for the uncommon grammatical option when the most common usage, to translate *kai* in the sense of "and", fits perfectly well.[51]

Secondly, for Paul to suddenly have inserted such a groundbreaking theological innovation in his letter's closing benediction, going against his common usage of the term Israel, is very unusual, indeed exceedingly unlikely. There is no other instance where Paul uses the term Israel to mean the Church – so to import this new meaning into this text goes against the biblical witness on this issue.

Finally, the context of the argument being presented in the book of Galatians does not favour this novel interpretation. In Galatians, the Apostle Paul is addressing the Gentile members of the Church who are being taught by a group called the Judaizers that they need to come under the Law of Moses to attain salvation, particularly by undergoing the act of circumcision. Paul argues at length that justification is by faith alone. Throughout the epistle he makes a distinction between two groups, circumcision and uncircumcision, meaning Jew and Gentile (2:7-9; 5:6). In the preceding verse to the "Israel of God" statement, Galatians 6:15, he argues that salvation is not about whether a person is circumcised or not, but whether he has been made a "new creation" through faith. So, in verse 16 he continues to refer to these two groups and proclaims a joint blessing upon them all, as having accepted the rule of salvation by faith alone.

The first group to have walked by this rule are the Gentile (uncircumcised) believers, and the second group are the "Israel of God" (the circumcision), Jewish believers who have properly understood that, although they are circumcised, their salvation is by grace through faith. Paul did this to highlight the drastic contrast between his doctrine and that of the professing Jewish believers and the Judaizers who were teaching a works-based salvation that was leading the Church astray – something that he abhorred (Galatians 1:6-9). In a letter that devotes a lot of time to attacking the beliefs of this Jewish group, Paul used the phrase "the Israel of God" to make it clear that he was not attacking those Jewish believers who correctly understood the gospel of Grace and were resisting the teaching of the Judaizers. This description was a fitting compliment for these Jewish believers.

In light of these arguments, there is insufficient evidence to justify the innovative assertion that, in Galatians 6:16, the Church is now referred to as the new Israel.

Romans 9:6

But it is not as though the word of God has failed. For they are not all Israel who are descended from Israel;

This is another verse that is sometimes used to prove that, theologically, the word Israel has been expanded to include believing Gentiles. However, such an understanding requires reading more into the text than it says. The distinction that Paul is making here is between those already inside the nation of Israel. The point is that within the ethnic nation of Israel some have accepted Jesus as their Messiah so have believed the gospel and been properly saved by grace, whereas others have not. Paul is not dividing between a spiritual Israel that incorporates all believers (i.e. the Church) and a carnal or earthly Israel, but between Jews who believe and Jews who do not.

The theological point is that, within the nation of Israel, there are still many who have not entered into the promised spiritual blessings given to them by God's covenant promise – a relationship implied by the name Israel. Therefore, it is quite proper for Paul to make the distinction that the believing Jewish remnant can in one sense be considered the true Israel, as they have inherited the divine promises. The Gentiles are not even in view in this statement and, as such, it therefore offers no support for the view (of replacement theology) that Israel has been broadened to include Gentiles (cf. Romans 11:1-5).

Galatians 3:6-9, 3:29

Even so Abraham believed God, and it was reckoned to him as righteousness. Therefore, be sure that it is those who are of faith who are sons of Abraham. The Scripture, foreseeing that God would justify the Gentiles by faith, preached the gospel beforehand to Abraham, saying, "All the nations will be blessed in you." So then those who are of faith are blessed with Abraham, the believer.

...

And if you belong to Christ, then you are Abraham's descendants, heirs according to promise.

These verses in Galatians are another way that replacement theologians argue for their version of theological identity theft. This time using the biblical teaching that believers are called "Abrahams sons" and "Abrahams seed". From these statements it is often argued that believing Gentiles are now spiritual Jews. The logic then follows that this new group of spiritual Jews together are a new spiritual Israel. However, such logic is faulty: even physically, not all descendants of Abraham are Jewish. The Arabs, who trace their lineage through Ishmael are equally descendants of Abraham, but they are definitely not Jews. The same is true in the spiritual sense: Gentile believers are indeed said to be the seed of Abraham, but this does not mean they are spiritual Jews.

We know from Romans 4:11-12 that Abraham is the father of all who believe, Jews and non-Jews alike. Therefore, in the context of the discussion in Romans what is meant by the expressions "sons of Abraham" and "Abraham's descendants" is this: just as Abraham was justified and declared righteous through his faith and not his works, so those who are true followers (or descendants) of Abraham are also justified by their faith. This is the focus of the discussion – not the formation of a new spiritual Israel comprised of the new spiritual Jews. Once again, the replacement theologians are taking too much away from the text to support their presuppositions. As Arnold Fruchtenbaum has stated, what "they need to prove their case once and for all is a statement that all believers are "the seed of Jacob"; this would go a long way to prove that the Church is spiritual Israel, or that gentiles are spiritual Jews. This is exactly what they do not have".[52]

Galatians 3:28, Colossians 3:11

There is neither Jew nor Greek, there is neither slave nor free man, there is neither male nor female; for you are all one in Christ Jesus.

...

a renewal in which there is no distinction between Greek and Jew, circumcised and uncircumcised, barbarian, Scythian, slave and freeman, but Christ is all, and in all.

These two texts shall be taken together as they represent another avenue of reasoning that is sometimes employed by replacement theologians to do away with a distinct or future role for national Israel. Rather than seeking to demonstrate that Gentiles are now the true Israel, here they have flipped it over; instead, they argue that there is now no distinction between Jew and Gentile, so those who continue to hold that distinction are going against the unity given to the Church through Christ. What do we make of this challenge?

To correctly interpret the meaning of the phrase "neither Jew nor Greek" and similar phrases in Scripture it is important to look at the entire context of the passages. It is true that in certain areas the distinctions between Jewish and Gentile believers have been taken away – but it is an altogether different matter to claim that any and every difference is now inconsequential.

The context of the Galatians text is justification by faith. Thus, in verse 24, the law is described by Paul as a tutor to lead us to Christ, "so that we may be justified by faith". Then again, in verse 26, he states that our position as "sons of God" has come to us "through faith in Christ". He continues by saying that all of us who have been baptized into Christ (i.e. saved by grace through faith) hold this new status. Having established these truths, Paul comes to the expression we are interested in, immediately claiming that there is neither Jew nor Greek, slave nor free, male nor female. So, quite clearly, he is not arguing that absolutely no distinctions exist, which would contradict so much of his other teaching, rather that, regarding the matter of salvation by faith, there is no distinction between these Jews and Gentiles – the only way of salvation is through faith in Christ.

Similarly, in Colossians the context of the discussion is to do with spiritual maturity and sanctification. The passage begins by listing characteristics of the old nature, the earthly body (v. 5), encouraging the reader to "put them aside" and to "put on the new self who is being renewed to a true knowledge... (v. 10)." Then, in verse 11, Paul writes that, in this renewal, there is no distinction between Greek and Jew etc. So, in its context the verse is saying that, regarding spiritual growth and Christian maturity, the process of sanctification in the life of a Christian, there is no distinction between the two groups of people; it is the same for everyone. Just because unity exists in areas that relate to salvation and spirituality, does not stop functional distinctions from existing elsewhere within the body.

Simply put, all that can be taken from these texts is that, with regards to salvation, growth and maturity of the Christian believer, God is no respecter of persons. Nothing more should be taken from them. To use this verse to argue that national Israel has no future is to pull these verses out of context and make them say something other than the Apostle Paul intended.

1 Peter 2:9-10

But you are a chosen race, a royal priesthood, a holy nation, a people for God's own possession, so that you may proclaim the excellencies of Him who has called you out of darkness into His marvellous light; for you once were not a people, but now you are the people of God; you had not received mercy, but now you have received mercy.

These verses demonstrate another line of argument often used by replacement theologians. The fact that Israel language such as "chosen race" and "holy nation" are being used in a New Testament epistle has been taken as evidence to support the idea that the Church is synonymous with Israel or that the concept of Israel has been broadened to include the Church.

Initially, it needs to be said that, even if New Testament believers are corporately addressed using Israel language, it does not follow that one people (the Church) has assumed another's (Israel) unique identity. The fact that Gentiles are also part of the people of God (having been "grafted in", Romans 11:17, 19, 23) – and in many ways share a similar function, witness and continuity with the people of Israel – means there is no reason why such language cannot be used in a way that illustrates certain common truths. So even if Gentile believers are being addressed here, it is not a definitive affirmation of replacement theology.

However, it is clear that looking at 1 Peter 2:9-10 within the wider context of the epistle, the focus is on Jewish believers living outside the Land of Israel amongst Gentile populations. The introduction to the letter identifies Peter's addressees as those "who reside as aliens", or as some translations have it, those of the "dispersion". This is a technical Jewish term – the Diaspora – for those who are not living in the Land of Israel but are residents of Gentile nations. The same phrase is also used in the book of James where he makes it even clearer, addressing the recipients of his letter as "the twelve tribes who are dispersed abroad" (James 1:1). Peter, then, is here writing to Jewish believers, the remnant of Israel. This view fits with Peter's calling as the apostle to the circumcision (Galatians 2:7-8) and it has the support of many commentators throughout Church history.

Peter is seeking to highlight the contrast between the remnant and the non-remnant of Israel with regard to national calling. In this chapter he identifies those members of the non-remnant of Israel as the ones who rejected the Messiah; Jesus was "the stone which the builders rejected" (2:7) and "a stone of stumbling and a rock of offense" (2:8). Peter uses Exodus 19:5-6 as a backdrop in order to highlight the believing remnant of Israel as "living stones" a "holy nation" and a "royal priesthood" (2:4-5), all terms describing the calling of national Israel. Peter is using this terminology to refer to the believing remnant to make the point that they have not failed in their calling and are offering up spiritual sacrifices to God as they "proclaim the excellencies of Him who called [them] out of darkness into His marvellous light" (2:9).This conclusion does not seek to deny that the "priesthood" of all believers, Jew and Gentile, is clearly taught in the Bible (Revelation 1:5-6), only that this particular grouping of expressions drawn from Exodus 19 have primary significance to the early Jewish believers.

Hebrews 8:13

When He said, "A new covenant," He has made the first obsolete. But whatever is becoming obsolete and growing old is ready to disappear.

This text illustrates another, rather muddled way that replacement theologians disinherit the physical promises of restoration from Israel. By pointing to this text, they are arguing that all the promises attached to the "old" covenant have been fulfilled with the coming of Jesus – therefore that covenant is now "obsolete". In so doing, they have in mind any promises that give a unique status to national Israel and that speak of a future regathering to a physical Land.

The problem is that no attempt is ever made to really define what is meant by the broad classification "Old Covenant", or to discuss it within the context of the other covenants specified in the Bible. There are four major covenants in the Bible: the Abrahamic covenant, the Mosaic covenant, the Davidic covenant and the New/Messianic covenant. All are found in both the Old Testament and the New Testament, indicating that we need to think more critically about the claims being used to make Israel obsolete. The main problem is the way in which replacement theologians conflate the Abrahamic and Mosaic covenants into one homogenous composite which they call the "Old Covenant". This leads to the vague but constant refrain that the New has replaced the Old in order to prove that the promises to national Israel no longer have any relevance today. But is this not exactly what Hebrews 8:13 says? This is where we need to carefully think through the argument step by step.

In the context of the entire book of Hebrews, the covenant to which the word "obsolete" specifically refers is the Mosaic covenant – which was always supposed to be temporary until the Messiah came. We can generally agree with the argument being put forward up to this point. However, there is a crucial problem to notice with this line of argument, as advanced by replacement theologians: they will then subtly add all the Land promises, which were part of the Abrahamic covenant, into the category of "old". This serves as justification for no longer accepting them as valid. Yet, this is not what the text in Hebrews says. Instead, it is speaking only of the Mosaic regulations. While the New Testament clearly teaches that the regulations for righteousness contained in the Mosaic covenant are terminated by Jesus, the Scriptures do not give such support for the abrogation of the Abrahamic covenant with the Jews. In fact, according to Galatians 3:17-18, Paul specifically refuted such a notion: "This is what I mean: the law, which came 430 years afterward, *does not annul* a covenant previously ratified by God, so as to make the promise void. For if the inheritance comes by the law, it no longer comes by promise; but God gave it to Abraham by a promise" (my emphasis). Therefore, any attempt to use Hebrews 8:13 to remove the promises from Israel is unwarranted.

Matthew 21:43

Therefore I say to you, the kingdom of God will be taken away from you and given to a people, producing the fruit of it.

This verse is used by replacement theologians to try to prove that the nation of Israel has been permanently rejected and replaced by the Church. When this verse is read through the lens of replacement theology it does appear to lend considerable support to the view that Israel has been rejected. However, such an interpretation is the outcome of reading later theological developments into the text. A proper examination of the verse within its immediate context does allow for alternative interpretations.

In this text Jesus is using the common Jewish symbol of a vineyard to represent the nation of Israel. This imagery is found in many places throughout the prophets. In Isaiah chapter five the prophet gives us the parable of the vineyard, which speaks of the vineyard (Israel) producing bad fruit and ultimately ending up being judged. Elsewhere Isaiah talks of a fruitful vineyard as a glorious future for Israel (27:2-5). This vineyard theme as an illustration of Israel is also found in Jeremiah (12:10-11) and Hosea.

Jesus builds upon this Old Testament imagery in His parable to show how the leaders of Israel have acted towards the ultimate Landowner. The parable is very direct: God the Father is represented as the Landowner who built the vineyard, which represents Israel proper. He rents it out to the vine-growers, who are the leadership of Israel. The slaves who are sent to receive the fruit are the prophets of Israel. Finally, the Landowner sends His Son, who represents the Messiah. The Son is killed, and God pronounces judgement upon this generation of vine-growers. Having told this parable (the meaning of which was certainly not lost on the religious leaders to whom it was addressed), Jesus makes His strong statement about the kingdom being taken away and given to another, fruit-producing nation.

It is important to note that the context is thoroughly Jewish throughout. There is no reason to suddenly think that this other group is the Church, which at this point it still an unexplained mystery of the New Testament to be revealed later. The three important issues to answer are: 1) who is the "you" that the kingdom is being taken from, 2) who is the "people" it is being given to, and 3) is the removal permanent. The best interpretation of the parable seems to be the one that builds upon the existing "vineyard" imagery of the Old Testament. That Israel would be judged at some point for killing the prophets and rejecting the Messiah but would ultimately still receive eschatological blessing. This seems to be the point Jesus is making when in verse 42 He quotes from Psalm 118; "The stone which the builders rejected, this became the chief cornerstone". Then he pronounces the removal of the Kingdom from the generation of Israel that rejected Messiah while He was on earth. It was the leadership of Israel that led the nation to reject the Messiah and, therefore, it was from them that the kingdom was being taken. They would now suffer the Judgement for rejecting the Messiah, which took the form of the destruction of Jerusalem in AD 70. This is confirmed when Jesus is seen lamenting over Jerusalem two chapters later in Matthew 23:37-39

> "Jerusalem, Jerusalem, who kills the prophets and stones those who are sent to her! How often I wanted to gather your children together, the way a hen gathers her chicks under her wings, and you were unwilling. Behold, your house is being left to you desolate! For I say to you, from now on you will not see Me until you say, 'Blessed is He who comes in the name of the Lord!'"

So, although there is judgement prophesied on Israel, the words of Jesus indicate that there will be a future group who will lead the nation in national acceptance of the Messiah when they cry out to the Lord with the phrase in Matthew 23:39. This helps us to identify the group referred to as "a people" in Matthew 21:43: it is those to whom the kingdom is given. The word "people" here is *ethnos*, often translated nation in the New Testament. This would seem to rule out the claimed identification of *ethnos* (by replacement theologians) with the Church because, technically, the Church is not a nation in this sense. To insert the concept of the Church at this juncture, that is a people called from every tribe tongue and nation, does not fit.

Rather the point is that, due to unbelief and rejection of the King Messiah, the kingdom was to be taken from that generation who would then go on to suffer the judgement of AD 70. There will however be a future generation, "a people" whose spiritual state will be one of repentance, that will cry out "blessed is He who comes in the name of the Lord", and this generation of Israel will gladly receive the Messiah and the Kingdom at that time. This seems to fit the flow and context best as well as making sense of the many passages that speak of a future national blessing for Israel (c.f. Romans 11:26).[53]

Conclusion

I acknowledge that not all of the subject matter of this book has been particularly pleasant to read – but it is essential that Christians in today's evangelical churches have a sound scriptural understanding of the Jewish people. The long history of Christian antisemitism needs to be acknowledged with tears and repentance, and any remaining roots of such thinking in the Church confronted. As has been demonstrated, the teaching of replacement theology has often contributed to this shameful legacy. It is imperative that the Church in our time stands against antisemitism in all its forms. Having a proper perspective on what transpired in history will help the Church ensure that such oppressive and cruel actions are not repeated under the banner of Christianity ever again. In the future, we must pray and take action to ensure that the Church sends a clear message that antisemitism is antithetical to true Christian faith.

Endnotes

1 Walter C. Kaiser Jr, An assessment of Replacement Theology: The Relationship between the Israel of the Abrahamic covenant and the Christian Church, *Mishkan 21*, 1994, pg. 9.

2 Michael J Vlach, *Has the Church Replaced Israel?* (Nashville: B&H Publishing, 2010) pg. 12.

3 Loraine Boettner, *The Millennium* (Philadelphia: Presbyterian & Reformed, 1957) pg. 89-90.

4 Origen, *Contra Celsus* 4:22.

5 Hippolytus, "Treatise Against the Jews", in *Ante-Nicene Fathers Vol. 5, Fathers of the Third Century* (New York: Cosimo Classics, 2007) pg. 220.

6 Melito of Sardis, *On Pascha,* trans. by S.G. Hall (Oxford: Clarendon 1979) pg. 21.

7 Darrell, Bock; Mitch Glaser. *Israel the Church and the Middle East: A Biblical Response to the Current Crisis* (Grand Rapids: Kregel Publications, 2018) Pg. 180.

8 Eusebius' *Ecclesiastical History*, trans. by C.F. Cruse (Massachusetts: Hendrickson Publishers, 1998) pg. 111.

9 Justin Martyr, *Dialogue with Trypho* 11.5.

10 Mal Couch (Ed), *Dictionary of Premillennial Theology* (Grand Rapids: Kregal Publications, 1996) pg. 39.

11 Luther's Works (35:287-88; WA, DB 11:400) quoted in: Michael Vlach, *Has the Church Replaced Israel?* (Nashville: B&H Publishing, 2010) pg. 57.

12 From his name we get the term for the theological system known as 'Calvinism.'

13 John Calvin, "Commentary on Daniel 2:44," *Commentaries on the Prophet Daniel.* trans. Thomas Meyers, 1852 (Albany: Ages Digital Library, 1998)

14 M. Phillips, Christians Who Hate Jews, *The Spectator*, 16 February, 2002.

15 Ibid.

16 Wistrich Robert S, *Anti-Semitism: The Longest Hatred* (Methuen Publishing Ltd, 1991).

17 Dennis Prager & Joseph Telushkin, *Why the Jews: The Reason for Anti-Semitism* (New York: Touchstone, 2003) pg. 75.

18 Eusebius, *Life of Constantine Book III*, Chapter XVIII.

19 S. Grayzel, Jews and the Ecumenical Councils, *The Jewish Quarterly Review* 57:287-311, 1967. doi:10.2307/1453498

20 Church Councils, *Encyclopaedia Judaica.*

21 Ibid.

22 James Parkes, *The Conflict of The Church And The Synagogue* (New York: Atheneum, 1974) Appendix 397-398.

23 Dan Cohn-Sherbok, *Anti-Semitism* (Gloucestershire: The History Press, 2009).

24 C. Brewer, The Status of The Jews In Roman Legislation: The Reign Of Justinian 527-565 CE, European Judaism: A Journal for the New Europe 38(2):127-139, 2005.

25 Cyprian, Three Books of Testimonies against the Jews *The Ante Nicene Library*, Eds. Roberts and Donaldson, (T. & T. Clarke, 1896) Treatise 12 vol. 13, pg. 23.

26 R. R. Ruether, *Faith and Fratricide: The Theological Roots of Anti-Semitism* (New York: Seabury Press, 1974) pg. 136.

27 John Damascene, An Exact Exposition of the Orthodox Faith, Book 4, chapter 23 in: *Against the Jews on the Question Sabbath.*

28 Fred Wright, *Words from the Scroll of Fire* (Jerusalem: Four Corners Publishing, 1994) pg. 104-105.

29 Augustine, *Exposition on the Psalms*, *Psalm* 59.

30 Ibid.

31 Edward Flannery, *The Anguish of the Jews* (New Jersey: Paulist Press, 1985) pg. 50.

32 Fred Wright, *Father Forgive Us: A Christian response to the Church's heritage of Jewish persecution* (Grand Rapids: Monarch Books, 2002) pg. 86.

33 Robert S. Wistrich, *Anti-Semitism: The Longest Hatred* (Methuen Publishing Ltd, 1992) pg. 3.

34 Attempts have been made to argue that the language is simply a strong rhetorical device used in polemical works at this time. Having read the entirety of The Jews and their Lies, I am unconvinced that there is anything to salvage from this work.

35 Martin Luther, On the Jews and Their Lies, from Luther's Works, Vol. 47 in: *The Christian in Society IV,* Ed. Franklin Sherman (Philadelphia: Fortress Press, 1971) pg. 268-72.

36 Paul Johnson, *A History of the Jews* (London: Phoenix Press, 2001) pg. 579.

37 Peter the Hermit was a leader in the so called "people's crusade" that actually left before the "first" crusade. The people's crusade was mainly farmers and peasants. Peter's preaching across Germany inspired other groups of crusaders, who were responsible for the Rhineland massacres in 1096.

38 The belief that the consecrated wafer actually becomes the host (from the Latin hostis, meaning victim), the very body of Christ, was the Catholic belief of transubstantiation that was believed at this time.

39 Edward Flannery, *The Anguish of the Jews* (New Jersey: Paulist Press, 1985) pg. 99.

40 In fact, as recently as 2014 an Arabic edition of The Protocols of the Elders of Zion was available on the Egyptian government's State Information Service website.

41 Jonathan Sacks, *Anti-Zionism is the New Anti-Semitism, Says Britain's Ex-Chief Rabbi*, Newsweek Opinion, 3 April, 2016.

42 Working Definition of Antisemitism, International Holocaust Remembrance Alliance. www.holocaustremembrance.com/working-definition-antisemitism

43 Phyllis Chesler, *The New Anti-Semitism: The Current Crisis and What We Must do About It* (San Francisco: Jossey-Bass Publishers, 2005) pg. 87.

44 The Coordination Forum for Countering Anti-Semitism, FAQ: The Campaign to Defame Israel. www.antisemitism.org

45 Paul Johnson, *A History of the Jews* (London: Phoenix Press, 2001) pg. 572.

46 Ibid, pg. 575.

47 Dan Cohn-Sherbok, *Anti-Semitism* (Gloucestershire: The History Press, 2009) pg. 264.

48 Natan Sharansky, 3D Test of Anti-Semitism, CFCA, 21 December, 2009.

49 In reality Israel receives a high rating by Freedom House that monitors civil and political freedoms of countries.

50 The NIV and RSV translate it this way. Translations such as the NLT are even more direct: "May God's peace and mercy be upon all who live by this principle; they are the new people of God."

51 M.R. Vincent, *Vincent's Word Studies in the New Testament* (Peabody, MA: Hendrickson, 1985) Vol 4. Pg. 180 – Vincent writes, "The explicative Kai is at best doubtful here, and is rather forced."

52 Arnold Fruchtenbaum, *Israelology: The Missing Link in Systematic Theology* (California: Ariel Ministries, 2001) pg. 702.

53 For a full treatment of Romans 11:26 please see book one, Thomas Fretwell, *Why Israel: Understanding God's Plan for Israel & the Nations*.

About the Author

Thomas Fretwell is the founder and director of the Ezra Foundation. He holds both B.Th. and M.A. Degrees in Theology and is currently undertaking Ph.D. research in a field related to Jewish-Christian Studies. He is a tutor in Theology at King's Evangelical Divinity School where he teaches courses on Israel, Politics, and the Land for the schools Jewish-Christian Study Centre. Thomas regularly speaks to people of all ages on a variety of biblical topics and apologetics issues. He hosts the Theology & Apologetics podcast and is the Pastor of Calvary Chapel Hastings in the UK.

EZRA FOUNDATION
STUDY ✡ PRACTICE ✡ TEACH